THE
DISCOVERY AND MYSTERY
OF A
DINOSAUR
NAMED
JANE

Judith Williams

Enslow Publishers, Inc.
40 Industrial Road
Box 398
Berkeley Heights, NJ 07922

*For our friend Jane,
in appreciation of her counsel and guidance in
revealing the fascinating lost world of Jane the dinosaur.*

Library of Congress Cataloging-in-Publication Data

Williams, Judith (Judith A.)
    The discovery and mystery of a dinosaur named Jane / Judith Williams. — 1st ed/
      p. cm. — (Prime)
    Includes bibliographical references and index.
    ISBN-13: 978-0-7660-2730-5 (library edition)
    ISBN-13: 978-0-7660-2709-1 (pbk)
    ISBN-10: 0-7660-2730-9 (library edition)
    ISBN-10: 0-7660-2709-0 (pbk)
    1. Jane (Tyrannosaurus rex)—Juvenile literature. 2. Paleontology—Hell Creek Formation—Juvenile
literature. 3. Paleontology—Cretaceous—Juvenile literature. 4. Vertebrates, Fossil—Hell Creek Formation—
Juvenile literature. 5. Tyrannosaurus rex—Hell Creek Formation—Juvenile literature. I. Title. II. Series.
QE862.S3W53 2006
567.912'9—dc22

                                        2006010475

Printed in the United States of America

10 9 8 7 6 5 4 3 2 1

To Our Readers: We have done our best to make sure all Internet Addresses in this book were active and appropriate when we went to press. However, the author and the publisher have no control over and assume no liability for the material available on those Internet sites or on other Web sites they may link to. Any comments or suggestions can be sent by e-mail to comments@enslow.com or to the address on the back cover.

Photo Credits: All photos © Burpee Museum.

Illustration Credits: Michael William Skrepnick, except map on p. 6 © 1999 Artville, LLC.

Cover Photo: Photo by M. Graham

JANE is a registered trademark of the Harry and Della Burpee Museum Association and is used with the permission of the association.

Table of CONTENTS

CHAPTER 1.

Prospecting for Fossil
Treasure, June 2001 5

CHAPTER 2.

Back to the Treasure,
June 2002 12

CHAPTER 3.

The Science of a Tyrannosaur 28

CHAPTER 4

Jane's World 39

Glossary 46

Further Reading and Internet Addresses 47

Index 48

A DINOSAUR NAMED JANE

JUNE 2001

The badlands of Montana are home to many fossils.

PROSPECTING
for Fossil
TREASURE
June 2001

Mike **Henderson** checks his watch, tapping it with impatience. It is still early in the day, but in two days his team will be returning to Illinois. Every minute brings them closer to leaving, but further away from finding a dinosaur. Grabbing his backpack, Henderson climbs out of the SUV, along with the rest of his team.

◇ 5 ◇

The Hell Creek Formation in Montana is home to many fossils.

Henderson's job is to search for fossils. He organized this trip for museum workers and volunteers from the Burpee Museum of Natural History in Rockford, Illinois. After two weeks of prospecting—hunting for fossils—they have found little more than small bone scraps and some teeth. Everyone hopes to be lucky enough to find a complete skeleton, but realizes that such a discovery is rare.

The team members scatter across the barren landscape. They are exploring a new area of the badlands in the Hell Creek Formation of Montana. This rock bed is known for its fossils. Henderson heads toward a hill, dry grass and shrubs crackling under his hiking boots. There are no trees, no shade, and no water. Henderson takes off his hat to wipe the sweat from his forehead. He walks quickly through the open flat area between hills because there is little hope of finding fossils on the ground there. Only the hillsides hold the evidence that dinosaurs once roamed these lands.

As the day passes, the chatter on the walkie-talkies increases. Scott Williams of the Burpee Museum smiles as the reports are radioed to him. This is turning out to be a good day for prospecting. Before long, discoveries include dinosaur leg and rib bones and a *Triceratops* horn. Scott Williams answers a radio call from volunteers Bill Harrison and Carol Tuck. Sensing the excitement in their voices, Williams turns and spies the pair in the distance. He hurries toward them, his rapid footsteps leaving dust hanging in the hot air. Minutes later Williams joins Harrison and Tuck at the base of a tall slope. A fossil sits on a little ledge of sandstone with other

*M*ike
*H*enderson

*S*cott
*W*illiams

bones nearby. Williams picks up the oddly shaped fossil, recognizing it as a toe bone. Behind it, there is another foot bone with the end broken off. He looks at it closely with wonder. The bone is hollow. Williams smiles widely at his team members. A hollow bone means a meat-eating dinosaur!

Almost a mile away, Mike Henderson steps carefully around a spiny cactus, closely checking for any sign of a dinosaur bone. Suddenly his walkie-talkie crackles, and the voice of Scott Williams breaks the silence around him. Williams radios that two volunteers have made a very interesting find. They agree to meet at the SUVs later in the afternoon.

The sun is low in the sky when the tired team assembles. Scott Williams holds out the fossil to Mike Henderson. As he handles the toe bone, the paleontologist's eyebrows raise in surprise and delight. He nods to Williams. No doubt about it. The hollow bone confirms the toe came from a meat-eating dinosaur. It is too late in the day to investigate the

site. As they drive away, everyone wonders what other bones might be hidden in the hillside.

The next day, Henderson crouches down to look at the ledge where Harrison and Tuck found the toe bone. He can see more still buried in the hillside. Farther along the slope, more bone and part of a dinosaur leg are partly visible.

The toe bone was the first fossil found from the mystery dinosaur.

◈ 9 ◈

Henderson walks beside the slope deep in thought. As his fingers trace the path of bones, a picture forms in his mind. If a dinosaur were lying down, its feet would be down at one end, and the leg bones would continue farther inside the hill. Henderson looks back and forth along the hill, too excited for words. The position of the bones could mean an entire dinosaur skeleton is lying right there in the hill beside them.

The paleontologist takes a second look at the toe bones. "These bones are too small for a full-grown tyrannosaur," Henderson says. "It might be a *Struthiomimus*." Both tyrannosaurs and *Struthiomimus* are meat-eating dinosaurs, known as theropods. Despite his doubts, he knows with certainty that the bones belong to a theropod dinosaur. Henderson sighs loudly. As exciting as finding a dinosaur might be, there is a problem.

The museum has a permit to collect fossils exposed on the ground, but not any bones that

require major digging. A large digging site would require another permit. There is no time to get one because they will be leaving for Illinois the next morning. The prospecting trip is over. Henderson tells the team they must leave the dinosaur in the hill. Everyone starts talking at once, concern in their voices. What if someone else finds this place and digs up the skeleton before they can come back?

The team removes the smaller exposed foot bones and buries the spot under rocks and dirt. This will hide their find from others and also protect the fossil from the weather until they return. The team members walk to the SUVs with one last, troubled look back at the slope. Are all the bones from a single theropod? Maybe even a tyrannosaur? The crew will have to wait another year to find out.

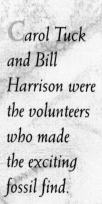

Carol Tuck and Bill Harrison were the volunteers who made the exciting fossil find.

Chapter 2

BACK to the TREASURE

June 2002

One **year** later, the Burpee Museum team returns to the Hell Creek Formation in Montana with written permission to dig. Nervously, the crew approaches the hill where they found the foot bones. Some of the loose rocks and soil they piled up to protect the fossil site have washed away. But the bones are still covered, and the crew sighs in relief. No one else discovered their find.

The mysterious dinosaur is still waiting for them, deep inside the hill.

The team sets up its headquarters at Camp Needmore. Often paleontology crews have to camp when they work in the badlands. However, Camp Needmore is only a one-hour drive from the fossil site. With cabins and hot showers, the camp is a welcome spot to return each night after a long day of digging in the hot sun.

Camp Needmore

Each day the team drives their three SUVs to reach the dig site, or quarry. This trip begins on the highway and follows a variety of back roads, each one worse than the one before. The last part of the trip takes the SUVs straight into the badlands where there is no road at all. With their insides still bouncing from the bumpy ride, the team unloads their gear. They pull out rock hammers, pickaxes, and shovels for heavy digging. For survival, they bring hats, walkie-talkies, food, and very large water bottles.

Henderson knows that the foot bones they found are about fifteen feet straight down from the top of the hill. To reach the level where the remaining bones may lie, the team must remove the top fifteen feet of the hill, called the overburden. Paleontologists always try to remove the overburden so they can dig from just above where they found a fossil. This allows them to carefully uncover the bones and then protect them. If they tried digging in from the side where they found the toe bones, parts of the hill might cave in. If that happened, the skeleton could be damaged.

Although it is summer, the Hell Creek site's high elevation makes mornings cool, sometimes even freezing cold. This changes quickly as the day goes on, with temperatures becoming blazing hot. On most sunny days the thermometer reads above 90 degrees Fahrenheit (32 degrees Celsius). The crew

Fossil bones appear on the side of the hill. Fifteen feet of overburden must be removed above the fossil.

swings the picks, digging hard while mosquitoes and black flies buzz around their faces. The work is hard and the hill is big. Even when they are hot and tired, the crew pays attention to the surroundings. Rattlesnakes live in this area, so no one can be careless.

Erosion from time and weather has worn away all the land that once surrounded this dinosaur grave. Because there is no grass covering the hill, the rock layers are visible along the side of the hill. The layers are different colors, forming stripes. Each stripe represents a period in history—thousands or sometimes millions of years. The layer holding the dinosaur is a different color from the layer above and below it, and is about thirty inches (seventy-six centimeters) thick. The striped rock layers make it easy for the team to know where to dig.

After three weeks, the team reaches the layer where they first found the dinosaur toe bones. Everyone slows down, removing the rock very

JUNE 2002

The team continues to expand the site.

carefully. No one wants to find bone and then break it by accident! Henderson and Williams work carefully in the dirt and rock layer. At the same time, they watch everyone else for a sign that someone has hit bone. The closer they get to the bottom of the layer, the more nervous they become.

Although the signs are promising of finding the entire skeleton, the crew knows it is possible they will find nothing more than the exposed bones they first saw on the side of the hill. But as they carefully scrape away hard rock, the fossils begin to show through. The team is now excited with the find. Is the skeleton complete? The answer is still unknown, but from what Henderson and Williams can see, a large part of it is

Once the team removed the overburden rock, they carefully uncovered the skeleton. This part of the skeleton shows the pelvis of the dinosaur.

present. The pair are relieved their hunch paid off. It would have been disappointing to clear away that much overburden for only a few limb bones.

The good news of reaching the bone layer is passed on to the Burpee Museum. Many famous dinosaurs have nicknames, and the crew learns that the director of the Burpee Museum has named this new dinosaur *Jane*. The name honors Jane Solem, who has made many generous donations to the Burpee Museum.

Henderson hopes the dinosaur bones will be arranged the same as when the animal lived, but soon it is clear that some of the bones are mixed up. This can happen for several different reasons. Once the dinosaur died, other animals could have fed on

it or walked over it, messing up the bones. It can also occur if moving water shifts the bones around once the dinosaur is dead. The team continues to dig, still hoping to find the most important part of the skeleton: the skull.

The Excavation

Surveying the Hell Creek site, Henderson realizes that the team needs help with the digging. The quarry site must be widened to make more room to work. This requires a great deal of rock to be moved. Every day is precious now; they do not have time to spend another three weeks taking down more of the hill. Henderson hires a backhoe driver. The driver brings his heavy digging machine to the site. Then with the team supervising, the driver uses the backhoe to remove more of the hill surrounding the quarry. Each time the backhoe scoops away rock, the team checks to make sure no bones have been touched. Soon, the heaviest work is done.

There are several jobs for the crew now that the site is expanded and many bones are visible. They start by drawing a quarry map. This is not like a road map. A quarry map is a drawing that outlines the shape and location of all bones in the rock. The team lays down a huge plastic sheet and then traces all the bones onto the plastic using a marker. This information is then copied onto paper.

Mike Henderson and Scott Williams organize some of the team to begin the excavation of Jane's skeleton. It would take too long to dig out every bone and bone fragment. Instead, they will dig out entire areas of rock, cutting them into blocks called slabs. To do this, the team checks where bone starts and stops. Then they begin to dig a trench around the edges.

A *map of the quarry shows the locations of all the bones in the rock.*

While some of the crew members dig around the slabs, others return to cleaning the visible bones. To clean away dirt, the crew uses small scrapers, picks, dental tools, brushes, and brooms. Exposed bones are covered with a liquid called Vinac. Once dry, it preserves the fossils and makes them stronger.

The hot sun beats down on the team members as they work shoulder to shoulder in the quarry. There is no shade and no wind to cool them. The "no-see-um" flies bite and bite and bite—making

*M*any small tools are used at the dig site.

Key:

A. large crate
B. small army surplus box
C. one-hundred-foot tape measure
D. paleo picks
E. plaster mixing bucket
F. paleobond
G. thermos

H. first-aid kit
I. field jacket
J. cold chisel
K. rope
L. work gloves
M. brushes
N. resealable plastic bag with fossils

O. burlap
P. small tools (picks, dental tools)
Q. small specimen cases
R. small paintbrush and toothbrush
S. rock hammer
T. pad of paper

A trench now surrounds the slab of bones.

everyone grumpy. Although the crew members take turns cleaning the bones and digging trenches, they tire quickly under the sizzling sun. The team decides to rig up a tarp to help shade the people in the quarry. While still hot under the cover, Mike Henderson enjoys the slight drop in temperature. And he wonders, *Where is the skull?*

Volunteer Brian Ostberg brushes the dirt from the area in which he is working. His hand stops in midair. His breath catches in his throat. He turns to the crew, calling out, "I've got a tooth!" Quickly Scott Williams joins him, and Ostberg steps back.

Williams is excited, but cautious, as he cleans away rock around the shiny brown tooth. Henderson kneels down to watch Williams work. Everyone else stops working and watches. Quickly and carefully, Williams cleans away more dirt. Suddenly, a row of very large teeth is showing. The lower jaw! Henderson and Williams examine the large, terrifying teeth as no one says a word.

"It's a tyrannosaur!" the two men yell. The team explodes with excitement, cheering and dancing around the quarry. Finding the skull is like discovering a chest filled with treasure. Everyone realizes that this dinosaur is very special because the jaw is too small to be a full-grown *Tyrannosaurus rex*. It is either a young *T. rex* or another species of tyrannosaur. Either situation is rare and a thrilling find for any museum. But for a small museum like the Burpee, Jane is the best kind of buried treasure.

July passes quickly, bringing with it a variety of weather that makes work difficult at times. When it

Jane's teeth were up to six inches long.

rains, mud sticks to everything. The area around the quarry becomes slippery and unsafe. The SUVs get stuck. On sunny days, the heat and bugs continue to bother the crew. Even the SUVs suffer as the jagged ground shreds the tires into hanging pieces of rubber. There is at least one flat tire every single day, but

nothing stops the crew. They are not going to wait another year to pull the fossil from the ground.

Protecting the Fossils

The most important job is to protect the fossils so they can be safely moved to the Burpee Museum. The team prepares the slabs, which contain the bones, for removal. They cover the sides and top of each slab with aluminum foil. Then layers of burlap strips soaked in wet plaster are added. The burlap dries hard and strong, protecting the fossil like the cast on a broken arm. Paleontologists call these plaster, burlap, and rock packages "plaster

Mike Henderson completes the plaster jacket for the lower jaw bones.

The team uses the backhoe to lift the jacket out of the ground.

jackets." Some bones, such as the lower jaw, are covered in plaster and burlap; they are small enough to be removed separately. Small, loose fossil pieces, like teeth, are put in little containers with foam called specimen cases.

By August, the four rock slabs containing Jane are covered in a solid layer of plaster. Combined, they weigh more than 2 tons. But 2 tons is too much for the team to lift onto the semitrailer truck waiting to transport Jane. The backhoe is called in to help again. The truck backs as close as it can to the quarry site, and then the precious slabs are carefully loaded onto the truck using the backhoe. Jane is strapped in for a safe trip.

The team waves good-bye to the drivers as the truck slowly pulls away from the quarry area. Jane's long trip from Montana to Illinois begins. The crew members shake hands with one another. They have wide, tired grins on their faces. The "little museum that could" just excavated its first major dinosaur!

Chapter 3

The SCIENCE of a TYRANNOSAUR

The fossils of an azhdarchid pterosaur were found with Jane.

Days later, when the truck pulls up to the Burpee Museum in Rockford, Illinois, a small crowd catches its first glimpse of Jane. The dinosaur from Montana has finally reached her new home.

Scott Williams organizes the team of staff and volunteers that will remove Jane from the rock. Their job is to clean Jane's skeleton so it can be displayed in the museum, but there is a lot of work to be done before that happens. First, the plaster jackets are opened so that several people can work at the same time. While everyone is excited to work on Jane, they are a little worried, too. The bones break easily, and most of the people have never prepared a dinosaur fossil before. Making it even harder, sometimes the bone looks just like the rock!

Preparing Jane for Study

The team uses many different tools to remove rock from the fossil bone. Some are power tools that do tough jobs like drilling through rock. In delicate or small areas of the fossils, workers carefully scrape the rock away by hand with old dental tools. The final cleaning is done with a power tool that blasts baking soda against the bone. This removes the last stubborn bits of rock but does not hurt the bone surface.

If a bone is broken, the team uses glue to repair it. They fill cracks with a special clay that dries hard. The glue and fillers make the bones stronger and

Scott Williams uses small tools to remove the rock from Jane's fossil. ➤

A microjack carefully removes small areas of rock.

stop the cracks from getting any larger. Many of the bones are in pieces. The broken pieces need to be put together to make a complete bone. Jane is one huge dinosaur puzzle!

When all the bones are repaired, they are covered with many coats of Vinac. This makes the bones stronger. Scientists need to be able to handle the bones without breaking them.

The Burpee Museum makes records of all of Jane's information. After each bone is cleaned, its measurements and where it was found are recorded. This helps scientists who study Jane to compare her to other fossils.

◈ 30 ◈

The staff then makes casts, or copies, of Jane's bones. Wet rubber is poured over each bone. When the rubber dries, it is peeled off. The dried rubber, called a mold, is now the exact shape of the bone. Next, a liquid plastic is poured into the mold. When the plastic hardens, it is removed from the mold.

Casts are useful in many ways. Scientists can look at the casts and see all the details of the fossil without worrying about handling the real bone and breaking it. Large fossils are very heavy. Casts are light, so they are easier to examine or move into

Mike Henderson measures one of Jane's bones.

different positions. Since all of Jane's skeleton was not found, casts are used to replace the missing bones.

This worker pours wet rubber to make a mold of Jane's pelvis.

Finally, all the bones are prepared and the casting is finished. The team starts putting the real bones and cast pieces together to assemble the skeleton. Almost half of Jane's bones were found, making Jane one of the most complete tyrannosaur fossils ever found. As the skeleton starts to take shape, Scott Williams totals all the hours everyone worked on the skeleton. Staff and volunteers spent more than 10,000 hours preparing Jane.

A few surprises are found within the rock where Jane was discovered. The team found evidence of plants as well as fossils from a turtle and a champsosaur

Steel rods hold real bones and casts of missing bones in place. They form Jane's skeleton.

(small prehistoric reptile). But the most exciting discovery found with Jane was bone from the spine of a pterosaur (prehistoric flying reptile). For Mike Henderson, "it was the prize in the Cracker Jack box."

The paleontologist returns to his office to think. After all the hours Mike Henderson worked in the hot sun digging Jane out of the quarry, and the many more as he cleaned her skeleton in the coolness of the museum, one mystery keeps going through his mind: *What kind of tyrannosaur is Jane?*

The Mystery of Jane

Jane *is* a mystery. When paleontologists study a newly discovered dinosaur fossil, they compare each bone to those of other dinosaurs. This information helps them determine what species

of dinosaur it is. Henderson is certain Jane is a tyrannosaur. Could the Burpee Museum dinosaur belong to the most famous tyrannosaur family of all, *Tyrannosaurus rex*? Jane's bones are too small to be a full-grown *T. rex*. Is she a young *T. rex* or some other species entirely?

Henderson compares Jane to *T. rex*. Jane has more teeth than an adult *Tyrannosaurus rex*. There are other differences, too. *T. rex* dinosaurs have large, wide snouts in a heavy skull. Jane's snout is long and narrow in a much lighter skull, much like another kind of tyrannosaur called *Nanotyrannus*. The skull of this dinosaur was found in the same area of Montana as Jane. Also, Jane's teeth are not the same as *T. rex* teeth, and there are more of them. Does this mean that Jane cannot be a *T. rex*? Is she a *Nanotyrannus*? Henderson considers one more possibility: Maybe a young *T. rex* had different features from an adult *T. rex*. Was *Nanotyrannus* really just a young *T. rex* and not a different species of tyrannosaur?

The News of Jane Spreads

As the Burpee's new dinosaur was being prepared, word of Jane spread around the science world. Before long, many paleontologists came to the Burpee Museum to study Jane. After measuring and comparing Jane to other tyrannosaur fossils, the visiting paleontologists gave their opinions to Mike Henderson. But scientists do not always agree. In this case, some believe Jane is an adult *Nanotyrannus*. Others believe Jane is a young *T. rex*.

Their opinions are important, but the final decision belongs to Mike Henderson. To help him decide, he reads scientific papers about tyrannosaurs. He visits other museums to look at their fossils, especially juvenile, or young, tyrannosaur specimens. One thing catches Henderson's attention: Jane's shoulder joint is different from that of an adult *T. rex*. At other museums he finds young tyrannosaur fossils with shoulder joints just like Jane's. Then one day, exciting new information about dinosaurs arrives at Mike Henderson's office door.

Dr. Greg Erickson, a reptile and dinosaur scientist, comes to speak to Mike Henderson. Erickson explains that he has found a new method for finding out the age of dinosaurs. He has discovered that alligator bones have growth rings, just as trees do. In trees, adding up the rings shows how old a tree was when it was cut down. In alligators, counting the rings shows how old the animal was when it died. Dinosaurs and alligators are distantly related on the family tree of animals. So, it is possible that dinosaurs could have growth rings, too. Henderson gives Erickson a piece of Jane's leg bone to study. After looking closely at the dinosaur bone with special equipment, Erickson concludes that Jane was 11 years old when she died. A full-grown *T. rex* is believed to be about 18 to 20 years old.

Mike Henderson carefully considers all the facts he has learned. Scientists must sometimes make decisions based on

A cross section of Jane's leg bone shows growth rings. These rings may help scientists determine Jane's age.

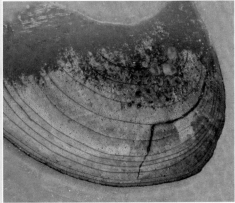

just a few animals until more specimens are discovered. Henderson knows that when more young tyrannosaurs are found, his opinion might change. But for now, he has all the information he needs to make his decision.

A DINOSAUR WITH A LIMP?

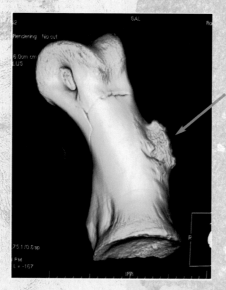

Museums sometimes take X rays of their fossils. When the Burpee Museum had X rays taken of Jane, something unusual was found. The test showed that Jane had an injury on a foot that had become infected. Looking closely, the scientists could see that one toe bone had a bony lump that was hollow inside. In life, that space would have been full of pus, the way the inside of a jelly doughnut is filled with jelly. Because bone grew all around the hollow of pus, the scientists know that the wound healed. No one knows how Jane got hurt, or if another animal attacked her. Although Jane's foot was probably painful even after it healed, she could still walk.

Chapter 4

JANE'S WORLD

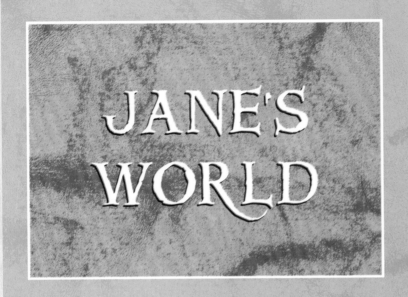

Champsosaurus bones were also found with Jane's fossil.

Close to 66 million years ago, Jane lived the life of a dinosaur at the top of the food chain. She was not full grown, but only had to worry about adult tyrannosaurs harming her. Jane's world was very different from the Hell Creek of Montana today. During different times of the Cretaceous period, an inland seaway covered this area.

◇ **39** ◇

By Jane's time the sea was slowly retreating, leaving rivers and plains that sometimes flooded. The land was richly covered with plants and flowers. In the latest Cretaceous, conifers (trees that bear cones, like the pine tree) were rare. Instead the forests were filled with shrubs and broadleaf trees like the sycamore and palm trees of today. The thick forest hid Jane as she looked for prey.

The most important part of daily life for a wild animal is its search for food. Jane was a meat eater. As a large animal, she would have needed lots of food. Did Jane hunt alone or in a group? Some paleontologists believe that tyrannosaurs lived and hunted in packs. If so, when Jane's foot was hurt, she may have eaten prey killed by her pack. But there is no way to prove whether she lived in a pack or not. If she was alone, Jane's injured foot may have made her a poor hunter. She may have had to eat dead animals she found instead.

How did Jane die? No one knows. She may have died during a flood, her body being washed downstream until it caught on a riverbank. Much of Jane's skeleton was found together. That means two things. First, other animals did not eat Jane after she died. Animals often grab meat and run off to eat it

Jane lived during the Cretaceous period, about 66 million years ago. "Jane's World" is the mural painting displayed at the Burpee Museum.

elsewhere. Second, it shows that Jane's body was buried quickly under sand and soil. Jane's watery grave actually protected her skeleton for the future. Now, 66 million years later, the Burpee Museum staff work hard to bring Jane and her world back to life.

The Museum Exhibit

The staff plans the exhibit that will be Jane's new home. Displays are made to explain how Jane was found and what her world was like during the Cretaceous period. A special team of workers mounts Jane's skeleton into an exciting pose. As Jane is assembled, Henderson realizes that visitors need more information to imagine Jane in her world.

Artists are brought in to help people see what Jane may have looked like. Tyler Keillor is a sculptor who will make a model of Jane's head. First, he makes casts of Jane's skull bones, creating extra cast pieces to replace the missing bones. After Keillor assembles the pieces into a life-size skull, he forms clay around it to make muscles and skin. He now casts the clay-covered skull, this time adding color to the plastic to make it look like skin. After removing the last cast from the mold, Keillor adds the eyes and paints the head, changing plastic into a real-looking dinosaur. Tyler Keillor steps back to check his work. Jane looks alive!

Michael Skrepnick is the artist who paints the mural of Jane in her world. He studies information about the plants and animals that lived in Hell Creek during Jane's time. Most important, he gets Jane's measurements to make sure he paints her correctly.

Tyler Keillor poses with his sculpture of Jane, as she may have looked when she was alive.

The artist then begins the painting of Jane. Skrepnick wants everything in the mural to be just as it was in Jane's time. "The plants, trees, the pterosaur in the sky, the champsosaur on the sandbar, and even the turtles on the log were all part of Jane's world," says Skrepnick.

◇ **43** ◇

Mike Henderson announces his decision: Jane is a young Tyrannosaurus rex.

The Treasure Revealed

Finally, everything is ready. On June 28, 2005, members of the press begin to fill the exhibit hall of the Burpee Museum. Mike Henderson stands before television, newspaper, and magazine reporters. The moment has come to solve the mystery of Jane. Henderson looks into the bright lights of the cameras and announces to the world that Jane is a young *Tyrannosaurus rex*.

A Glimpse of a Lost World

After the news conference, Mike Henderson looks at the new exhibit and remembers how luck and hard work made Jane's world come to life. Henderson closes his eyes for a moment. Suddenly Jane's skeleton transforms into a fierce dinosaur. She roars loudly—then limps through the trees, disappearing into the forest . . . and into our imaginations.

The Jane: Diary of a Dinosaur *exhibit at the Burpee Museum.*

GLOSSARY

badlands—A dry area of barren hills and valleys worn down by weather over time.

cast—A copy of a fossil.

Cretaceous period—A period of time, 144 to 65 million years ago.

erosion—The process of weather wearing down landforms.

fossil slab—A large block of rock and dirt containing fossils. The slab is covered with plaster so it can be safely moved.

Hell Creek Formation—Fossil-bearing hills in parts of Montana, Wyoming, and North and South Dakota. This fossil layer was formed 67 to 65 million years ago.

overburden—The rock and soil that must be removed to reach a fossil.

paleontologist—A scientist who studies fossils and ancient life.

prospect—To search for fossils.

quarry—A dig site where people work to remove fossils, historical objects, or rock.

species—A group of animals that share similar features. *T. rex* is one kind of species.

specimen—An example of something. A fossil specimen can mean an entire skeleton or part of one.

theropod—A kind of dinosaur that usually eats meat and walks on two hind legs.

FURTHER READING

BOOKS

Holtz, Thomas R., Jr. *T. Rex: Hunter or Scavenger?* New York: Random House, 2003.

Keiran, Monique. *Albertosaurus: Death of a Predator*. Vancouver: Raincoast, 2000.

Tanaka, Shelley. *New Dinos*. Toronto: Madison, 2003.

INTERNET ADDRESSES

The Burpee Museum of Natural History
http://www.visitjane.com

The Children's Museum of Indianapolis. *Dinosphere.*
http://www.childrensmuseum.org/dinosphere/profiles/bucky.html

The National Geographic Society. *National Geographic Kids.*
http://www.nationalgeographic.com/ngkids/0005/dino/

INDEX

A

alligators, 37–38
artists, 42–43

B

backhoe, 19–20, 26, 27
badlands, 4, 13–14
Burpee Museum, 6–7, 12, 18, 23, 27–28, 30, 35, 36, 44
    exhibit, 42–45

C

Camp Needmore, 13
casts, 31–32, 43
champsosaur, 32, 34, 39, 43
Cretaceous period, 39, 42

E

Erickson, Greg, 37–38
erosion, 16
excavation, 19–25
exhibit, 42–45

G

growth rings, 37–38

H

Harrison, Bill, 7, 8
Hell Creek Formation, 6, 12, 15, 19, 39, 43
Henderson, Mike, 5–10, 14, 17–19, 21–23, 25, 31, 34–38, 42, 44–45

I

Illinois, 5, 6, 10, 27, 28

J

Jane
    age, 37–38
    death, 41–42
    hunting, 40
    injury, 40
    jaw, 23, 27
    name, 18
    shoulder joint, 36
    skull, 19, 22–23, 35, 42
    teeth, 23–24, 27, 35
    toe and foot bones, 7–12, 14–16

K

Keillor, Tyler, 42–43

M

measurements, 30–31, 43
molds, 31–32
Montana, 6, 12, 27, 35, 39

N

Nanotyrannus, 35, 36

O

Ostberg, Brian, 23

P

paleontologist, 8, 10, 14, 25, 34, 36, 40
plants, 32, 40, 43
plaster jacket, 25, 27, 29

preparation (fossil), 29–33
prospecting, 6, 7, 10
pterosaur, 28, 34, 43

Q

quarry, 14, 19, 21, 22, 25, 27, 34
quarry map, 21

S

skeleton, 15, 17, 19, 28, 32, 34, 41, 42, 45
Skrepnick, Michael, 43
slab, 21, 25, 27
species, 23, 34–35
Struthiomimus, 10

T

theropod, 10, 11
tools, 14, 16, 21, 29–30
Triceratops, 7
Tuck, Carol, 7, 8
turtle, 32, 34, 43
tyrannosaur, 10–11, 23, 28, 32, 34–36, 38–40
Tyrannosaurus rex, 23, 35, 36, 38, 44

V

Vinac, 21, 30

W

Williams, Scott, 7–8, 17, 21, 23, 28, 30, 32